CW00794311

The People's History

Fence Houses, Lambton, Burnmoor & Chilton Moor

by

Lena Cooper & Geoffrey Berriman

Fence Houses Signal Box with Mr Thompson the signalman, *circa* 1930.

Previous page: The staff of Fence Houses Palace Cinema, *circa* 1913.

Copyright © Lena Cooper & Geoffrey Berriman 1999

First published in 1999 by

The People's History Ltd
Suite 1
Byron House
Seaham Grange Business Park
Seaham
Co. Durham
SR7 0PY

ISBN 1 902527 54 2

No part of this publication may be reproduced, stored in a mechanical retrieval system, or transmitted, in any form or by any means, electronic, mechanical, photocopying, recording or otherwise, without prior permission of the authors.

Contents

This book is dedicated by Lena Cooper to her sister-in-law Dorothy Dawson and also in memory of her brother William Dawson who appears in the photographs, and by Geoffrey Berriman in memory of his parents Alan and Frances Berriman who also appear in the photographs.

PROGRAMME

3-45 p.m.   Musical Programme by the Orchestra under the direction of R. Culbertson.

4-15 p.m.   Arrival of HER ROYAL HIGHNESS THE PRINCESS ROYAL at the Fence Houses Y.M.C.A.

Civic, Y.M.C.A. and other Special Guests will be presented, and the New Building inspected.

4-30 p.m.   The National Anthem.

Prayer of Dedication by the Reverend E. G. Casey, the Vicar of Chilton Moor Parish Church.

4-35 p.m.   Welcome to Her Royal Highness by Councillor B. A. Bircham, J.P., Chairman of Houghton-le-Spring U.D.C., on behalf of the Urban District Council and the Citizens of Fence Houses.

4-40 p.m.   Mr. Alan Berriman, T.D., Chairman of Fence Houses Y.M.C.A. will welcome Her Royal Highness on behalf of the Association.

4-45 p.m.   Remarks by The Rt. Hon. Viscount Lambton, M.P.

A page from the programme for the opening of Fence Houses YMCA New Building by HRH the Princess Royal on Tuesday 25th March 1958.

Introduction

The photographs we have included in this book should help to show the diversity of the district. Although associated strongly for many years with coal mining, agriculture has always played a prominent part, and since the end of the Second World War there has been a programme of factory building to accommodate new industry.

The district can boast a castle and several manor houses, churches and chapels of different denominations, and it also played a prominent part in the early development of the railways.

We expect that there are many more photographs of the area and its people which we have not seen, and we hope that the owners will retain these as part of an important record of the area.

Believed to be the opening of the Pit Head Baths, Lambton D Pit, late 1930s.

Acknowledgements

In preparing this book we have been fortunate in the generosity of many people who have provided photographs and postcards.

We wish to give particular thanks to Mr George Nairn for supplying cards and photographs from his substantial collection, and for always being generous with his time and expertise. We should also like to give special thanks to Mr Bob Jones for not only providing photographs, but for allowing us to make use of his research on Fence Houses Station.

We should like to thank the following for providing photographs, and their readiness to help:
Mr & Mrs Morgan Hardy, Mr Alan Yardley, Mr John Taylor, Mr Stephen Watson Hardy, Mr & Mrs Callan Hope, Mr & Mrs Bill Beattie, Mr Derek Beattie, Mrs Olga Patterson, Mrs Ellen Wilson, Mr Norman Pimlett, Mrs Jean Cornish, Mrs Miriam Oliver, Mrs Ethel Thompson, Mrs Judith Lees, Mr & Mrs Ernest Clark, the Vicar and P.C.C. of St Andrew's, Chilton Moor, Mr Wilf Burrows, Mr Tom Davis, Mr & Mrs Osman, the headteachers of Burnmoor and Dubmire Schools, Mr Robert Maddison and Mr David Maddison, Mr G.W. Stowes, Mr B. Chater, Mr Peter Robson, The Misses P. & N. Soppitt, Mr Alf Roxby, Beamish Open Air Museum, Tempest Millennium Photography, North East Press and Durham County Fire Brigade.

We wish to thank Mrs Carole Brown for her work in transcribing the text.

The authors would also like to acknowledge the assistance from Mr Bob Laverick, Chairman of the Dubmire Branch of the Royal British Legion.

We pay tribute to the pioneering work of the late Mr Ken Richardson in producing photographic histories of the area.

An outing of people from Colliery Row at the beginning of the twentieth century. Mr Alf Hales, organist at Colliery Row Chapel, is front right.

SECTION ONE

BURNMOOR AND LAMBTON CASTLE

The village of Burnmoor, or Bournmoor as it is now sometimes spelt, has always been associated with the Lambton family, and many houses were built by the Lambton Estate in the village. This photograph, taken *circa* 1905, shows estate houses roofed with clay pantiles, a form of roofing which was quite common then, but few examples of which remain in the district today. The houses on the right were known as Long Row, and no longer exist.

This is another view of Long Row at Burnmoor, probably also taken at the beginning of the twentieth century.

Taken *circa* 1905, this is a very rural view showing the Church of St Barnabas, Burnmoor, on the right, and the Church Lodge, centre background.

This photograph, taken *circa* 1930, shows in more detail the Lodge near Burnmoor Church. Note the fine lamps on the brick pillars at the Lodge gate. Of the lamps, only the bases remain.

Burnmoor Church Lodge & Rectory 13777

This excellent photograph, probably taken in the 1930s, shows from the left: the Rectory (now The Old Rectory), the Lodge, and the Church.

The Parish Hall at Burnmoor. This fell into disrepair and was demolished in the late 1970s. The new houses forming Church Close were built on the site.

Taken *circa* 1910, the picture shows Burnmoor Church School which later became the home of Burnmoor Cricket Club who still use it today. The building on the right also still stands. Now a private house, its name 'The Old Post Office' recalls its former purpose.

Taken *circa* 1905, this picture also shows the old Post Office. The Post Office also became known locally as 'Wylam's Shop', this name coming from the family who ran it and who also sold groceries. The cottages on the right have long been demolished.

This photograph, taken in 1999, shows how little the building has changed. Note the post box on the gable end.

BOWES' HOUSE, BURNMOOR.   JC

Taken in the 1920s, these buildings in Lambton Park are very much the same as today. Note the railway track to the right which was used to haul heavy goods into the estate from the main road, and was dismantled many years ago.

BURNMOOR FROM SIXTH PIT

A scenic view taken of Burnmoor from the heights of Sixth Pit, *circa* 1920. The church can be seen in the background. High Primrose Hill shown in the foreground still stands today. There has been much housing development since this photograph was taken.

Another more detailed view of the High Primrose Hill Cottages, *circa* 1905.

In the early 1970s the cottages became derelict, but were renovated in 1974, and are shown in this 1999 photograph.

Several modern shops serve the community of Burnmoor. Here is Arlington Stores in 1999.

For many years one of the High Primrose Hill Cottages was a police house, and a well-known occupant was PC George Nairn shown here with his dog Trix.

A large amount of house building took place in Burnmoor between the 1960s and the 1990s including the houses at Ellesmere (above) built in the 1960s, and the houses at Castlemain Close (below) built in the 1990s.

The Gardens at Lambton Castle.

This photograph of Lambton Castle was taken in the early part of the twentieth century before demolition work in the 1930s considerably reduced the castle in size. The castle was originally designed in the early nineteenth century by Ignatius Bonomi for the first Earl of Durham.

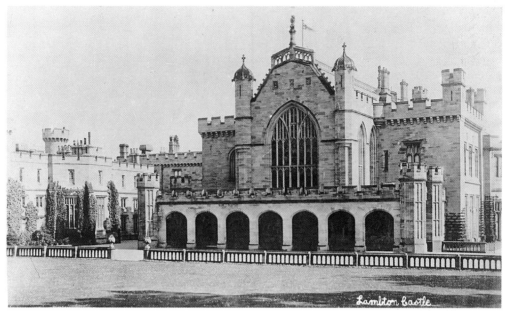

This view of Lambton Castle, also taken before the demolition in the 1930s, shows the Great Hall which was designed by Sidney Smirke, the son-in-law of the great Newcastle architect John Dobson who also carried out design work on the castle.

This photograph, probably taken in the 1950s, when it was used as an adult education college by Durham County Council, shows the Castle in its much reduced state.

Biddick Hall is a fine early eighteenth century house in the grounds of Lambton Park. Although in private use, the house has generously been made available by the Lambton family for many charitable fund-raising events.

Biddick Hall Lodge, *circa* 1905. The building no longer exists.

The small hamlet of Houghton Gate near Burnmoor, *circa* 1905.

Houghton Gate in 1999. The only surviving house from the period when the 1905 photograph was taken is the end house at the right of the picture. It is believed that the other houses were demolished shortly after the 1905 photograph, although until the late 1950s there was a house in the scrub and woodland area shown at the front of the modern photograph, which was lived in by Mrs Gadd, the widow of a former rector of Burnmoor.

The Dun Cow Inn at Bournmoor was shown on the first Ordnance Survey Map of 1854, and probably has a history going well beyond that. It has been sympathetically added to in recent years.

The Bungalow at Burnmoor. The date and location are unknown. Does any reader have the answers?

SECTION TWO

BRECON HILL, LUMLEY THICKS, SIXTH PIT, WOODSTONE VILLAGE AND NEW LAMBTON

The walk through Brecon Hill Woods between Floaters Mill and Castle Dene has long been a local favourite. There is always a wonderful display of bluebells in May. For many years the water in the stream was badly polluted, but in the early part of the twentieth century it was often used for bathing.

Most of the buildings shown on this photograph, *circa* 1905, have long gone, and Brecon Hill is a much smaller settlement today. Lumley Bridge Forge is shown in the foreground.

This photograph taken in 1999 shows two of the remaining buildings at Brecon Hill. The Smith's Arms on the left has been a public house for at least 150 years. On the right is Lumley Forge Farm.

This photograph taken in 1999 is of the old Methodist Chapel at Brecon Hill, now converted into houses. It was last used as a chapel in the 1950s.

The attractively situated hamlet of Lumley Thicks in 1999.

This photograph, also taken in 1999, shows the former Chapel at Lumley Thicks, now converted into a house which is appropriately called the Old Chapel House. Note the similarity in style between this building and the Old Chapel at Brecon Hill (page 23).

Floaters Mill Farm at the beginning of the twentieth century. It then had a clay pantile roof.

Mr Anthony Langton, left, and Mr Thomas Langton Jnr, sons of Mr Thomas Langton, shown here in 1960, continued farming at Floaters Mill.

Mr Thomas Langton in retirement. Mr Langton became the farmer at Floaters Mill in 1927.

This is another view of Floaters Mill Farm, *circa* the late 1930s. The village of New Lambton can be seen in the background to the right. By this time the clay pantiles on the farmhouse had been replaced by slate. The barn to the left was still pantiled.

In the early 1980s farming ceased at Floaters Mill, and the farmhouse is now the Poacher's Pocket public house and restaurant, shown here in 1999.

In the summer of 1999 extensive repair work was being carried out to the bridge over Floaters Mill stream. In this photograph a grain trailer has a puncture on the bridge, and the police have just arrived. The police officer on the left is walking up to the photographer to ask him very pleasantly why he is taking a photograph. She was satisfied with the explanation that it was for this book.

The photograph shows a much more serious incident when a bus was involved in an accident at Sixth Pit level crossing in 1924.

The Miners' Welfare Hall at Woodstone Village, *circa* 1938.

The Welfare Hall building, shown here in 1999, is now Fence Houses Community Centre. The railway tracks shown in the older photograph have gone, and the road is much wider.

Woodstone Terrace, shown here in 1999, is a typical example of the red brick and slate roof terraces built in the area at the beginning of the twentieth century. These particular houses have the advantage of good sized gardens, and rural views to the rear.

Mr & Mrs J. Pattinson outside 21 High Row, Woodstone Village in 1943.

Fence Houses Fire Brigade in front of Sixth Pit in the early 1960s. Some of the firemen were local men who worked as firemen on a part-time basis.

Fence Houses had its own fire station from the early 1960s until the late 1990s. The building is now called Woodstone House, and is a depot for Home Group Limited.

This picture, taken in 1999, shows the site of the former Lumley Brickworks. In the mid-background there can just be seen a surviving brickworks chimney. At one time there were many brickworks in the area because of the large deposits of clay. This site is now being developed for housing.

Mill Row at New Lambton, *circa* 1910, since demolished. Does any reader know the purpose of the structure on stilts to the right of the row?

Another street at New Lambton, *circa* 1910. Note the families standing outside their front doors to the right.

Local residents outside Railway Terrace, New Lambton, *circa* 1964. Lambton Colliery is in the background. Railway Terrace was demolished in the early 1970s.

Barry Richardson at the rear of Railway Terrace, New Lambton, *circa* 1964.

The old railway bridge and pedestrian tunnel at New Lambton, 1999.

This photograph, taken in 1999, shows one of the cottages at New Lambton known as Aged Miners' Homes which were built in 1937.

Panfield Terrace, New Lambton, 1999. As with other houses in this street the house at the extreme right has retained its original small coal house door at the front.

FENCE HOUSES

A view showing Morton Grange Terrace on the left, Gill Crescent in the centre, and Sydney Street to the far right, *circa* 1912. The original photograph is entitled Break Neck Gill. The spot deserves its name as it has been the scene of numerous traffic accidents over the years when vehicles have failed to take the bend carefully.

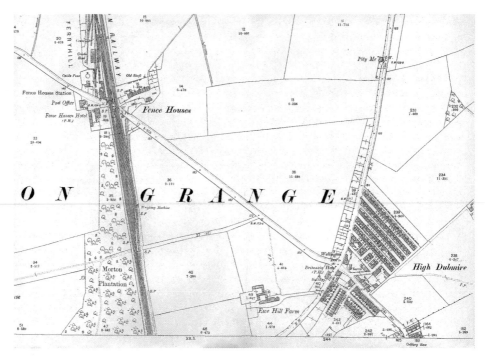

This extract from the second edition of the Ordnance Survey Map 1896
should be compared with the extract from the third edition (1920) below.
By 1920 there had been considerable additional building on both sides of
the railway line. (Reproduced from the 1896 Ordnance Survey Map.)

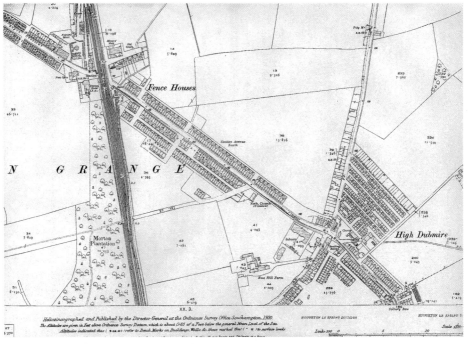

Reproduced from the 1920 Ordnance Survey Map.

A 1948 advertisement for
T. Morton, Baker, Fence Houses.

In 1966 the gill in front of Morton
Grange Terrace flooded making access to
Morton House impossible. For several
days canoeists were able to take
advantage of the conditions. The gill was
culverted by Chester-le-Street Council in
the early 1970s.

Accommodation at Cedarwood, Fence Houses, built for senior citizens in the
early 1970s.

Gill Crescent South, Fence Houses, in 1905 before the building of the streets behind and Gill Crescent North. Corner shops were often included at the end of a street or a section of it, and the shop windows of number 20 can be seen centre left. Number 20 currently forms the premises of Alter-It who carry out clothing alterations.

Mrs Hall and Mr Jimmy Tate at the back of Maplewood Street, Fence Houses. Billy Beattie sits on Mr Tate's knee while Mrs Morgan looks on from next door, 1953.

Mr Derek Pimlett holding the Chester-le-Street Grammar School Victor Ludorum trophy, *circa* 1965. In the background is New Briarwood Street.

This bonfire was built on the recreation field to mark the Coronation of the Queen in 1953. Pinewood Street is shown to the left, and Maplewood Street to the right.

A view of Morton Grange Terrace to the left, the Gill Crescents to the centre, and South Crescent to the right, *circa* 1925. This can be compared with the 1999 photograph below of much the same scene.

Mr Isaac Berriman beside his home, The Woodlands, Fence Houses, with his eldest son Ronald and his daughter Ethel in 1912.

Workmen outside the joinery workshop of Isaac Berriman, Building Contractors, *circa* 1928. South Crescent can be seen in the background.

Mr Alan Berriman (middle) with two members of the staff of Isaac Berriman outside the Woodlands Joinery Works, 1928.

A well-known shop in South Crescent was that of F. Tower, Newsagent, *circa* 1914.

Another well-known shop was A. Nesbitt's Sweet Shop in Morton Crescent, *circa* 1925. This was also later run as a sweet shop for many years by Miss M. Pratt.

One of the remaining shops in Fence Houses today is Ainsworth's Foodstore shown here in 1999. A previous business at the premises was the Meadow Dairy, Grocers.

A 1999 view of South Crescent with the Oakwood Residential Home on the right. The home stands on the site of Fence Houses Palace Cinema which subsequently became a bingo hall before being demolished. (See page 115.)

A view of Co-operative Terrace, Fence Houses with the signal box in the background, *circa* 1910. This photograph was taken before the building of Morton Crescent on the right hand side of the road.

Another view of Co-operative Terrace and the Fence Houses branch of the Chester-le-Street Co-operative Society before the building of Morton Crescent on the opposite side of the road. The store and the 12 houses of Co-operative Terrace were built in 1904.

Mr William Dawson of Fence Houses in his grocery jacket and apron in 1935 when he worked at the Co-operative.

The modernised grocery department of the Fence Houses branch of the Chester-le-Street Co-operative Society, *circa* 1937.

Fence Houses Post Office to the left with Morton Crescent in the centre, and the Co-operative building on the right, *circa* 1920.

A 1999 photograph from a similar angle. The Post Office was demolished in the early 1960s, and a garage was built on the site. On the extreme right can just be seen the lean-to building which can also be seen in the bottom photograph on page 44.

A smaller new Post Office was built on the opposite side of the road to the original building. This photograph, taken in 1999, shows the postmaster, Mr Jim Richardson (centre) with members of staff Mrs Helen Wilson (left) and Ms Joyce Powney (right).

Fence Houses Auction Mart, *circa* 1960. The Auction Mart was adjacent to the Railway Station, and was a well-known mart in the area.

Morton House in 1966. There was a manor at Morton centuries before the
present building was erected in 1709. The 1709 house originally had three
storeys (see photograph below) but there was a serious fire in the late
nineteenth century, and the top storey was removed. It was a private house
until 1988 when it was acquired by the Arnott Group as their headquarters.

This picture, taken in 1999, shows Lambton Lane with Lambton Miners' Hall on the right. The hall was erected by Durham Miners' Association in 1912. After the closure of the local colliery in 1965, it was used for some years as a sports hall by the YMCA. It is now used for business purposes. There are two houses attached on either side, North House and South House, and originally these were lived in by colliery officials.

Lambton Lane Garage in 1999 with the partners Mr Alan Dickinson and his son David.

STATION AVENUE, FENCE HOUSES. (765)

A tram running in Station Avenue, *circa* 1920.

This photograph, taken in 1999, shows Avenue Vivian on the Grange Estate which was built as part of Houghton-le-Spring Urban District Council's local authority housing programme in the decade after the end of the Second World War.

CHILTON MOOR, COLLIERY ROW, BANKHEAD AND DUBMIRE

Mr Parkin's Craftworks at Fatherly Terrace, Colliery Row, *circa* 1890. The Fatherly Terrace of that time has been demolished, but some modern housing also called Fatherly Terrace was subsequently erected.

Dubmire Cottages in 1999. These cottages are some of the oldest buildings in the Fence Houses area, although a number of modern alterations have been carried out over the years. When the photograph was taken, the owner of the middle cottage was carrying out some repairs, and these revealed the original stonework.

In the 1930s much of the older housing was demolished and there was a large local authority building programme which included houses such as these in Morley Terrace.

Included in the 1930s building programme were bungalows for elderly people like this one in Cedar Terrace.

After the end of the Second World War, English Industrial Estates constructed new factories at Dubmire. The factory on the left was one of the earliest built.

Factory building has continued on the Dubmire Industrial Estate, and this 1999 photograph shows factories of more recent construction.

This photograph shows a mix of old and new. The ducting and building form part of the Rexam Combibloc Factory on the Sedgeletch Industrial Estate. In the background can just be seen one of the remaining buildings of Lambton D Pit. The horses on the left are happy with their grazing.

Front Street, Bankhead.

Front Street, Bankhead, *circa* 1900. The building in the background on the right is the Wellington Inn. Some of the buildings on the near right also survive, and they include those that today house M. Lilley Newsagents, and the Popular Discount Store. We have not been able to identify the building on the near left, although the building back left is the former Britannia public house.

This 1999 photograph should be compared with the scene above.

This modern photograph also shows the Wellington Inn which was probably an old coaching inn.

A crowd outside the Wellington, *circa* 1920.

Bank Head, Fence Houses.   7075

A picture of Bankhead, *circa* 1925. The shop on the far left is now the Golden Fry Inn, and the shops to the right form the Edinburgh Bakery.

This 1999 photograph is of Dr Thomas' Harvesters Surgery which is opposite the Wellington. It was formerly the Britannia public house.

Front Street, Bankhead, looking south, *circa* 1900. Some of the buildings shown have been demolished, but the houses on the right still stand, and the Free Gardeners public house and the Londonderry Arms can be identified on the left.

The same view of Front Street, Bankhead, today.

On the right the Bankhead branch of the Newbottle and District Co-operative Society Limited, *circa* 1963. The building now houses the B & S Superstore (see below).

Above: Working in the allotment behind Britannia Terrace, Bankhead, 1999.

Make the most of your shopping
Shop at —————————————

GEORGE GRAHAM
LIMITED

THE PEOPLE'S STORES

1/6 in £ DIVIDEND 1/6 in £

SPEND AND SAVE

DEPARTMENTS

Grocery	Bakery
Butchering	Greengrocery
Readymades	Joinery
Drapery	Undertaking
Millinery	Blacksmith

Suits Made to Measure

Branches :
HOUGHTON - LE - SPRING
HERRINGTON BURN—WASHINGTON
RAINTON — CHESTER - LE - STREET
GILL CRESCENT—RYHOPE

Head Office :

FENCE HOUSES
THE PEOPLE'S STORES

Above: A horse drawn delivery vehicle of Graham's Stores in the late 1940s.

Left: A 1948 advertisement for George Graham Limited.

The hardware department at Graham's Stores, *circa* 1910.

The butcher's at Graham's Stores, *circa* 1910.

The Free Gardeners in Front Street is another long established public house.

At the entrance to the Old Church Hall (now the British Legion) at Dubmire, *circa* 1950.

Mr Tom Davis of Front Street, Fence Houses, well-known band leader in the area (see page 108).

Mr David Maddison (left) and Mr Robert Maddison in their traditional Cobbler's Shop, Front Street, Chilton Moor, in 1991.

The Londonderry Arms, Chilton Moor, in 1999. The Londonderry Arms was shown in this position on the first edition Ordnance Survey Map of 1854, but it would appear that the original building was replaced, as the style of the building in the photograph is later, probably *circa* 1900.

Chilton Moor House was the seat of the Chilton family in the sixteenth century. Although there have been a number of alterations over the years, it remains a very fine building.

Avon Crescent, built in the 1930s as part of a large local authority house building programme, stands on the site of the former Long Row. In the middle of this picture, taken in 1999, children can just be seen holding a jumble sale in their front garden.

Redburn Row near the burn of that name at Chilton Moor. While some of the building is later, and some of the original houses have probably been demolished, this row is shown on the first edition Ordnance Survey Map 1854. At the time it was adjacent to the Chilton Moor Brick Field, which was one of a number of brickworks operating in the area. Note the new tree planting in the foreground.

Mrs Pat Robson and (left to right) her children Carol, Peter Annette and Patricia on Black Boy Road, Chilton Moor, *circa* 1958. Mrs Robson's husband, Dr Bill Robson, was a well-known GP in the area.

Mrs Lilian Soppitt in the kitchen of 3 Durham Street, Fence Houses, *circa* 1926.

THE COLLIERIES

The history of the Durham Coalfield has been, and will continue to be, much researched in view of the importance of coal mining as a major industry. The last two pits in the area, Lambton D and Sixth closed in the 1960s, but there are still many men living in the area today who worked there. Most people of the age of 45 or more who lived in the area at the time will have their own memories of the mining industry and those who worked in it. This picture shows miners at Sixth Pit, probably shortly before it closed.

Miners of the Lambton collieries, *circa* 1890.

The Lady Ann and D Pits at New Lambton, *circa* 1900.

Building work at Lambton D pit, *circa* 1900.

The Old Engine at New Lambton. This was partly demolished and the ruins left for many years until subsequently removed when the site was landscaped.

Lambton Collieries Loco No 17 0-4-0 Saddle Tank built in 1873 by Hudswell, Clarke and Rodgers of Leeds.

Miners from Sixth Pit in training for the Mines & Rescue Brigade, 1937.

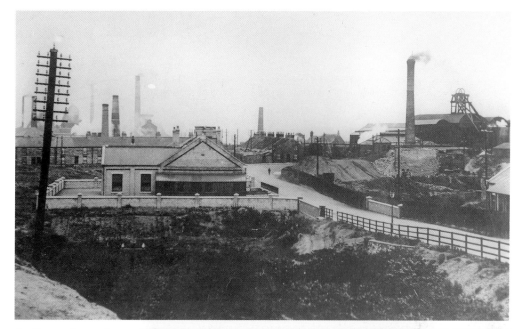

A view of Lambton D Pit on the right with Lambton Cokeworks in the background, *circa* 1920. Lambton Swimming Baths is on the left foreground. Note how close the houses were to the collieries.

Miners at Sixth Pit waiting for the cage to take them to work, *circa* 1950.

Members of the Lambton Lodge marching with the Lodge Banner on the main road in Fence Houses between Gill Crescent North and Gill Crescent South, *circa* 1937.

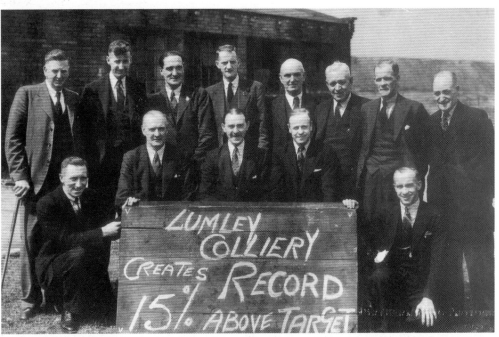

Officials of Sixth Pit proudly display a large notice announcing that the Colliery had created a record in 1944. The officials include: Messrs George Henderson, Frank Taylor, Arthur Oliver, Arthur Vardy, Henderson Lowerson, Bert Arnold, Rowe, R. Willis, Curry, and Mr Day, Manager.

A crane removing the pulley wheel at Sixth Pit on the closure of the colliery in 1965.

A 1999 photograph showing the remaining buildings of Lambton D Pit on the right, next to the new factory of TKT Cosyfoam Limited which provides local employment.

A 1980s view from Henry Terrace shortly before the demolition of Lambton Cokeworks in the background. Henry Terrace was named after the earlier adjacent William Henry Pit. In the photograph below the main chimney has just been demolished.

THE RAILWAY

Fence Houses Station was built in connection with the Newcastle and Darlington junction line, which provided a through route from York to Gateshead. The through route was inaugurated in 1844 and Fence Houses Station dates from that time. The station was demolished around 1964, but due to the need for main line diversions the line survived for another thirty years, and was often in heavy use at weekends. This photograph was taken around 1910.

Another view of the station from the north, *circa* 1910.

The level crossing looking up towards Station Avenue, *circa* 1910.

Fence Houses signal cabin looking north, with its original straight stairs. The Colliery lines are on the right.

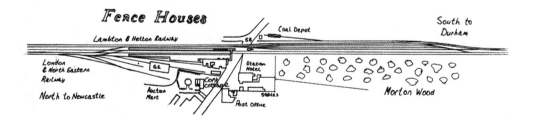

A plan of Fence Houses Station drawn by Mr Bob Jones of Burnmoor.

Fence Houses Station with steam train drawing, *circa* 1957.

Fence Houses Station during demolition in the mid 1960s. The footbridge has already been dismantled. The signal box was to remain for another thirty years before it was demolished after youths attempted to set fire to it.

The Station Hotel at Fence Houses seen from the railway line looking west in 1979. The Station Hotel is one of the oldest surviving public houses in the area.

The Fence Houses station master, Mr Dunning, with his grandson, *circa* 1954.

Taken from the site of the station in the late 1970s, this photograph shows left, Cork Cottage built in 1879; the octagonal shaped cattle Auction Mart centre; and the original goods yard building on the right. Cork Cottage and the goods yard building survive today.

The Auction Mart shown in more detail, 1979. It has since been demolished.

The WH Smith bookstore at Fence Houses Station, *circa* 1948.

Far right, Mr Harry Anderson at Fence Houses Station in the 1940s. Mr Anderson was manager of the WH Smith bookstore.

A view of the signal cabin at Wapping, Burnmoor, *circa* 1905.

Taken in 1999 outside Morton Wood, Fence Houses, looking northwards, this photograph shows how nature is taking over the disused lines.

SCHOOLS

Class 3 Dubmire Junior School in 1950. We hope that many of the former pupils shown in this photograph and others will be able to recognise themselves.

Burnmoor Boys School Group IV, *circa* 1905.

Burnmoor Girls School Group IV, *circa* 1905.

Burnmoor Schools

Auty Series. G.H. N/C 4657

The former Church Schools at Burnmoor. Since the 1930s the building has been a Club House for Burnmoor Cricket Club.

The former Lambton School is now used by Burnmoor Community Association. The photograph is *circa* 1920.

Fence Houses Senior Mixed School, *circa* 1935. The building now houses Woodlea Primary School.

Fence Houses Senior Mixed School Class 3, 1951. The headmaster, Mr Kirkbride, is pictured back row extreme right.

Burnmoor School in 1999. Penshaw Monument can just be seen background left.

Class 1 with the Egg Tree at Burnmoor School, 1999.

A class at Chilton Moor School, 1946. The school closed in the 1970s, and the building is now owned and used by Ho'ton Heating, Heating and Plumbing Engineers.

A teacher at Dubmire School with her class at their Harvest Festival display, 1951.

Dubmire Junior School in 1999. The school is a familiar landmark to many people who drive through Fence Houses. It was founded in 1914, and the clock, which can be seen in the photograph, was installed in 1953 to commemorate the Queen's Coronation. It is anticipated that the building will be replaced by a new school within the next few years.

Year 6 outside Dubmire School, 1999.

A recent class at Dubmire Infants School which is a modern building adjacent to the Junior School.

Year 3 Woodlea School, Fence Houses, 1999.

CHURCHES AND CHAPELS

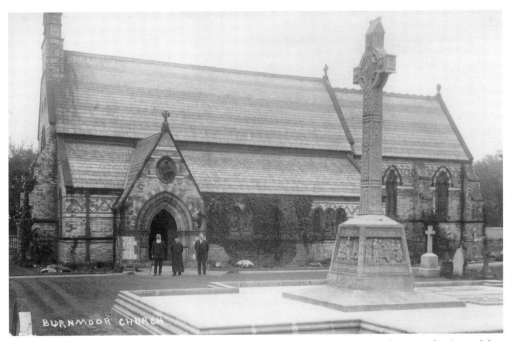

The Church of St Barnabas, Burnmoor, *circa* 1920. The church was designed by R.J. Johnson and was dedicated on 25th February 1868. The first rector was the Revd Alfred Merle Norman who was a Fellow of the Royal Society.

A page from the Order of Service for the institution of the Revd Arthur John Gadd as rector of St Barnabas' Church, Burnmoor in 1922. Mr Gadd was rector until 1951. He had served as a chaplain to the Forces in the First World War, and was known for his ability to keep the attention of congregations listening to his sermons. He was a literary man, and would sometimes compose poems in memory of parishioners who had died.

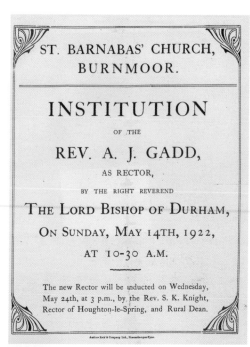

ST. BARNABAS' CHURCH, BURNMOOR.

INSTITUTION

OF .THE

REV. A. J. GADD,

AS RECTOR,

BY THE RIGHT REVEREND

THE LORD BISHOP OF DURHAM,

ON SUNDAY, MAY 14TH, 1922,

AT 10-30 A.M.

The new Rector will be inducted on Wednesday, May 24th, at 3 p.m., by the Rev. S. K. Knight, Rector of Houghton-le-Spring, and Rural Dean.

Andrew Reid & Company Ltd., Newcastle-upon-Tyne.

The Rev Malcolm and Mrs Bishop outside St Barnabas' Church. Mr Bishop was Rector from 1985-1997. He was a greatly loved and respected priest wherever he served and was actively supported throughout his ministry by his wife, Eileen. However, it was in the Parish of St Barnabas and the Burnmoor community that he was happiest and where many remember him 'as one of us – not just our Rector, but our friend.'

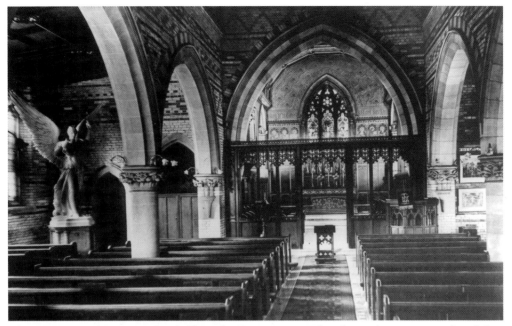

The interior of St Barnabas' Church, Burnmoor. The decor is an example of the Arts and Crafts movement of the time, and the church includes three stained glass panels by the celebrated firm of Morris & Co. The Angel of Victory, which can be seen on the left in the nave, was carved by Waldo Storey RA, and formerly stood in the Great Hall of Lambton Castle.

Probably taken in the Church Hall at Burnmoor in the 1940s. The rector, Mr Gadd, is third left, and Mrs Gadd is on the extreme right. On the extreme left is Mr Austin Kirkup who was for many years the managing director of the Lambton, Hetton and Joicey Collieries.

Members of Burnmoor Church Mothers' Union in the late 1940s. Viscountess Lambton is pictured centre front row with Mrs Gadd on her right. Other members in the picture include: Mesdames Gray, Watson, Adamson, Coulson, Thornton, Combey and Fennell. Mrs Fennell was the wife of the long serving church organist, Mr Frank Fennell, and she owned a millinery business in Fence Houses.

The wedding of Miss Ann Tiplady and Mr John Slack at Burnmoor Church in the late 1930s.

St John's Methodist Church, Station Avenue South, Fence Houses, in 1999. Many older residents will remember the previous church on this site which was known as the Tin Chapel, as it had been built with metal sheeting. It was painted a distinctive green.

New Lambton Primitive Methodist Church, *circa* 1910. The building no longer exists, but until relatively recent times had a strong congregation.

New Lambton Primitive Methodist Sunday School, *circa* 1916. The school was winner of the Christian Endeavour Shield which is shown in the photograph. The Sunday School Superintendent, Mr Edward Hind, is pictured in the back row. Margaret Dixon, who is also in the photograph below, is centre, middle row.

New Lambton Primitive Methodist Church in the early 1950s. Mr Edward Hind, who is in the photograph above, is shown at the back in front of the church door. Margaret Dixon, by this time Mrs Yardley, is second left.

The other chapel at New Lambton was the Wesleyan Church shown here in about 1910. It has also been demolished.

Below: This is a rear view taken in 1999 of the Bankhead Independent Methodist Church which is one of the older Methodist churches in the area still in use.

WESLEYAN CHURCH, NEW LAMBTON.

St Andrew's Church, Chilton Moor, 1999. With the growth of the mining industry many new churches were built in the latter half of the nineteenth century. St Andrew's was designed by George Gilbert Scott Jnr, and was begun in 1876.

The vicar of Chilton Moor, the Revd J.H. Shore and choir in 1930.

St Andrew's, Chilton Moor, Infant Sunday School in 1959. The teachers include: Mrs Hall, Mrs Hardy and Miss Forster.

The St Ceciliatide Music Festival at St Andrew's Church, Chilton Moor, 1960. The vicar, the Revd H.N. Swinburne, is centre back row, On his left is the well-known BBC North-East newscaster, Mr Tom Kilgour, and on his right is Mr R.M. Rogerson, the organist and choirmaster. At the far left, front row, is Mr George Goodyear, tenor, and on the far right, front row is Mr Alan Berriman of Fence Houses who was an accomplished classical violinist. Mrs Hazel Thompson, contralto, from Burnmoor, also performed in the festival.

The Revd Piers Davey, vicar of St Andrew's, Chilton Moor, from 1995, outside the vicarage in 1999.

Below: The Wesleyan Church, Colliery Row, which was built in 1872.

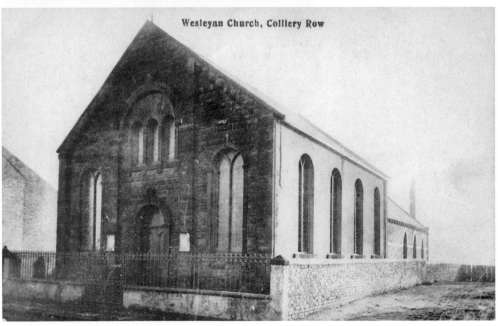

Wesleyan Church, Colliery Row

The interior of the Wesleyan Church, Colliery Row.

The Wesleyan Church Building, Colliery Row, as it is in 1999. Use as a chapel ceased some years ago, and the building is now used for storage. The street to the right of the chapel is North View Terrace.

The wedding of Flying Officer Bernard Lodge and Miss Joan Blight, both Dental Surgeons at St Andrew's Church, Chilton Moor, 1957.

ST. BARNABAS CHURCH

BURNMOOR

ON SUNDAY, JUNE 23RD, 1929

AT 10-30 A.M.

THE UNVEILING & DEDICATION

OF THE STATUE

THE ANGEL OF VICTORY

(dated Roma 1894, Sculptor, Waldo Story, R.A.)

BY THE RIGHT REVEREND

THE LORD BISHOP OF DURHAM

AND THE RIGHT HON.

THE EARL OF DURHAM

To the Glory of God and in Loving Memory of John George, Third Earl of Durham, K.G., born June 19th, 1855, died September 18th, 1928; also his twin brother, Frederick William, Fourth Earl of Durham, born June 19th, 1855, died January 31st, 1929. Given to Burnmoor Parish Church by John, Fifth Earl of Durham.
"Death is swallowed up in Victory."

An extract from the service sheet for the unveiling and dedication of the statue 'The Angel of Victory' at St Barnabas' Church, Burnmoor, 1929. It was in this year that the statue was moved from Lambton Castle to the church. The dedication of the statue was in memory of the Third and Fourth Earls of Durham, who were twin brothers, and who died within five months of each other.

THE FIRST AND SECOND WORLD WARS

It has been difficult to find photographs relating to the district during the periods of the First and Second World Wars. By the time of the Second World War more people had acquired cameras, but film was scarce and anyone who took a lot of photographs would have been looked upon with suspicion. Like all other parts of the country during these times men and women of the district, whether in military or civil occupations, made a significant contribution to the war effort, and this chapter of the book is dedicated to them. This photograph, probably taken early on in the Second World War, is of an air raid shelter which has been sand-bagged. Does anyone remember the precise location?

LAMBTON PARK CAMP, CHESTER-LE-STREET.

A military camp in Lambton Park during the First World War. A number of regiments were encamped at Lambton, including the Shropshire Yeomanry, the Cheshire Yeomanry, and the Scottish Horse. The camps contained up to two thousand men.

UH   LAMBTON PARK CAMP, CHESTER-LE-STREET.

Fence Houses Ladies Committee, Soldier and Sailors Sewing Party, 1914. The photograph was taken in front of Lambton House, the home of the Lambton Colliery Manager, Mr Jacob Sharp. Mrs Sharp is at centre, back row. Her sister, Mrs E.M. Berriman, is on her right, and on her left is her stepdaughter, Miss Ethel Sharp.

In 1916 Mr Jacob Sharp died, and Mrs Sharp subsequently decided to enlist. She became an officer in the Women's Army Corps, and is shown third from right, back row.

Private John Sinclair of Fence Houses who was in the 18th Battalion Durham Light Infantry.

This picture shows some of the medical and nursing staff who worked at the Long Room Military Hospital, Chilton Moor Farm.

Mr William Oliver of Fence Houses, middle row, centre. Mr Oliver joined the Tyneside Scottish and was attached to the Black Watch. He was captured early on in the Second World War and was a POW in Stalag 20B, Poland. He won a Geneva Convention award for his contribution to sports. In civilian life he was prominent in the revival of Durham County Show.

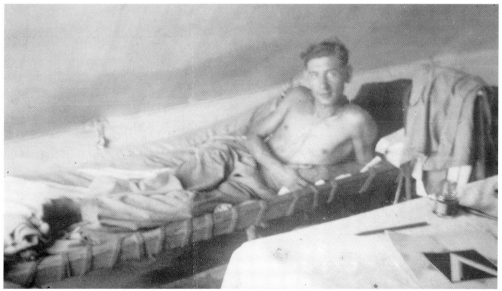

Mr Wilf Burrows of Fence Houses served in RAF Transport Command. He is shown here in a field hospital in India, *circa* 1944.

Mr Tom Davis of Front Street, Fence Houses, served in the RAF Air Dispatch Letter Service. He also played the tenor saxophone in a RAF band, and is shown second right whilst playing at RAF Northolt in 1944. On this occasion the Prime Minister, Winston Churchill, was in the audience. Mr Davis' unit landed in Hamburg on the day the war in Europe ended, and he was present at the surrender of the Luftwaffe. After the war he formed his own band. (See page 63.)

Mr Alan Berriman of Fence Houses, sixth left second row, as a Troop Commander in the Royal Artillery in 1941. He later served in North Africa and Italy reaching the rank of Major. He was awarded the Czechoslovakian Medal of Military Merit First Class for his war services.

Mr William Dawson, who was in the Royal Electrical & Mechanical Engineers, outside Burnmoor Church after his marriage with Miss Dorothy Wright in 1940.

Mr Dawson shown in his uniform as a Staff Sergeant. He served with the 8th Army in North Africa.

Above: Miss Mary Cain of South View, Chilton Moor, in her ATS uniform, 1944.

Above right: Miss Emily Robinson of Morton Crescent, Fence Houses, in the uniform of the Women's Auxiliary Police Corps during the Second World War.

Right: Mr Alf Roxby, well-known barber of Front Street, Fence Houses, who served in the Royal Navy.

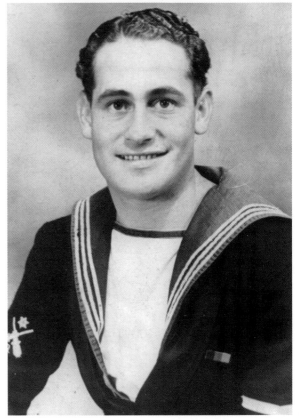

LEISURE, VOLUNTARY ACTIVITIES AND CLUBS

Volunteers of the Lumley and Burnmoor Division of St John Ambulance at Sixth Pit, *circa* 1934.

Bankhead Albions Association Football Club, winners of the Durham Amateur Club Trophy, *circa* 1912. The president of the Club was Mr Jacob Sharp, the Lambton Colliery Manager.

Chilton Moor Ladies Cricket Team versus The Gentlemen, *circa* 1912.

The successful Burnside Club Football Team, *circa* 1948.

Burnside Junior Football Team, 1963.

Another football team picture outside Lambton House, the home of the Colliery Manager, Mr Jacob Sharp, who was also president of the club, and is pictured in the inset second left. It was an indication of the importance of the Colliery Manager in the community that he was invited to be the president of sports clubs. Lambton House is now the Lambton House Residential Care Home.
Back: J. Elliott (goalkeeper). Standing: W. Coulson, W. Hall, Jn Towers.
G. Elliott, E. Dawson, I. Walby, J. Oliver, J. Parker, E. Taylor, Jas Burns,
R. Finlay, R. Gray, R. Stephenson and W. Rutherford, Seated: T. Langton
(Financial Secretary), S. Stavers (Chairman), R. Hall, I. Dunn, J.C. Round,
Jn Turnbull (Vice-president), Jn Dunn, T. Cherry, G. Laughton, J.M. Devonport
(Vice-President) and Anty Elliott (Assistant Secretary). Front row: A. Winship
(Trainer), Jn Winders, N. Brown and Jas Winship (Trainer). Inset: Jas Winder
(Captain), J. Sharp (President), Jn Dailey and Jn Dobson.

Fence Houses Modern School, Durham Schools County Cup Winners, in the 1950s.

Music pupils of Mrs F.J. Harrison at a concert performance held in Fence Houses YMCA in the late 1940s.

Fence Houses Palace Cinema in 1988 shortly before it was demolished. After the cinema closed the building was used as a bingo club. Oakwood Residential Home now occupies the site (see page 43). In the photograph the original projector room can be seen.

Burnmoor Cricket Club Pavilion, *circa* 1905.

A match in progress at Burnmoor Cricket Club in 1999. The imposing Cricket Club building is in the background.

Fence Houses YMCA was housed in these huts along Lambton Road before the new building was erected in 1957. Avenue Vivian is the street behind, and in the background left can be seen part of Lambton Cokeworks.

Fence Houses YMCA had an active Women's Auxiliary which acted as a social organisation, and which also raised funds for the YMCA. This picture is of the Women's Auxiliary's 1960 Summer Garden Party at the Woodlands, Fence Houses. Seated far left is the vicar of Chilton Moor, the Revd H.N. Swinburne; second left, Mrs T. Bancroft, the wife of the managing director of Lumley Brickworks; standing, Mrs Frances Berriman, President of Fence Houses Women's Auxiliary; and far right, Miss H. Seaton who was a teacher at Dubmire Junior School.

The 1971 Fence Houses Women's Auxiliary Summer Garden Party held at
Morton House, Fence Houses, the home of the President of the Auxiliary, Mrs
Frances Berriman, centre rear. Note the summer hats, and also the fine
doorway of Morton House.

The cast of *The Boyfriend*, a Fence Houses Amateur Operatic Society
production in 1962 at the Welfare Hall, Woodstone Village.

The district has a number of well-established clubs and associations. Burnside Workingmen's Club is situated between Gill Crescent North and South Crescent.

Well-known as the Comrades Club, this club behind Station Avenue North, was founded by Servicemen of the First World War.

Dubmire Workingmen's Club Committee, 1959. Back row: M. Hann, D. Alderson, R. Ayre, B. Shields, R. Lawton, F. Greenwell, R. Passmoor. Front row: E. Robson (steward), Mrs D. Robson, G. Hood (chairman), J. Nicholson (secretary), A. Roxby, M. Scurfield.

Dubmire Branch of the Royal British Legion at Britannia Terrace, Fence Houses.

Pigeon racing has long been a popular pastime. This picture of pigeon lofts near Henry Terrace, Fence Houses, was taken in 1999 from the railway line.

The First Burnmoor Cubs & Scouts with their leader outside their new marquee in 1997.

St. HILD'S COLLEGE BUILDING FUND

PROGRAMME

GLANTON SINGERS   Conductor: K. Hicks

    Yugoslav Folk Songs -   - *Matyas Seiber*

IAN BONAS—Pianoforte

    Prelude and Fugue—E major -   -   *Bach*
    Bk. 2 No. 9
    Fantasie Impromptu -   -   *Chopin*

MICHAEL CLEAVER—Bass Baritone

    Bois Epais -   -   -   -   *Lully*
    To Music -   -   -   *Schubert*
    False Phyllis -   -   *H. Lane Wilson*

ALAN BERRIMAN—Violin
WENDY SALLINGER—Violin
FLORENCE WILSON—Viola
BARBARA ORTON—Violoncello
Quartet in B flat major, K458, Opus 17 - *Mozart*
               (The Hunt)
    Allegro vivace assai
    Menuetto moderato
    Adagio
    Allegro assai

GLANTON SINGERS   Conductor: K. Hicks

    Diversions

SALLIE SPICER—Pianoforte
JOHN SPICER—Violoncello
ALAN BERRIMAN—Violin
Pianoforte Trio in E flat major, Opus 1 No. 1 - *Beethoven*
    Allegro
    Adagio Cantabile
    Scherzo
    Presto

End of Concert

Supper

During the ownership of Mr & Mrs Alan Berriman, Morton House (see page 48) was made available on many occasions to raise funds for causes in the Durham area. This was the programme for a concert held in 1970 to raise funds for St Hild's College, Durham. Mr Berriman played in this concert.

Playing dominoes in the Recreation Hut (now demolished) at the bottom of Gill Crescent South in the 1970s.

In 1999 the walks through
Brecon Hill Woods (see page
21) remain popular.

Local amenities for children
include this playground
adjacent to Woodlea School,
Fence Houses.

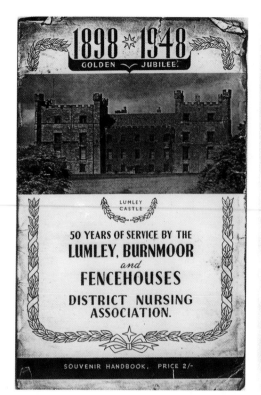

Queen's Nurse NEAL, 1923-1937

Queen's Nurse MUTER, 1937-1940

Queen's Nurse McQUE, 1940-1942

Queen's Nurse JOHNSON, 1942-1946

The cover page from the Golden Jubilee programme of the Lumley, Burnmoor and Fence Houses District Nursing Association. The Association was a voluntary one founded by the Dowager Countess of Scarbrough. In 1948 its work was taken over by the National Health Service.

Above right: Burnmoor Nurses of the Association. Money to pay the nurses was raised from collection and donations. Coal for the nurses was supplied free of charge by the Lambton, Hetton and Joicey Collieries Ltd and later by the National Coal Board.

Right: A programme for a bazaar held in the Welfare Hall, Sixth Pit, in 1931 to raise money for the Lumley, Burnmoor and Fence Houses District Nursing Association.

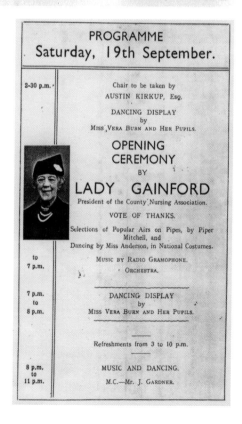

PROGRAMME
Saturday, 19th September.

2-30 p.m.

Chair to be taken by
AUSTIN KIRKUP, ESQ.

DANCING DISPLAY
by
MISS VERA BURN AND HER PUPILS.

OPENING CEREMONY
BY
LADY GAINFORD
President of the County Nursing Association.

VOTE OF THANKS.

Selections of Popular Airs on Pipes, by Piper Mitchell, and
Dancing by Miss Anderson, in National Costumes.

to
7 p.m.

MUSIC BY RADIO GRAMOPHONE.
ORCHESTRA.

7 p.m.
to
8 p.m.

DANCING DISPLAY
by
MISS VERA BURN AND HER PUPILS.

Refreshments from 3 to 10 p.m.

8 p.m.
to
11 p.m.

MUSIC AND DANCING.
M.C.—MR. J. GARDNER.

A Christmas party for Cedarwood residents, 1970s.

A sale of work in Cedarwood Communal Hall, Fence Houses, in the 1970s.

Harvesting linseed in Fence Houses, 1999. Ridgewood is left background. The Woodlands Joinery Works is to the right. This is a view taken from the bridleway running down from Morton House to Fence Houses.

Joe's Pond at Rainton Meadows, Chilton Moor. Formerly known as Nicholson's Pond, it was renamed after Mr Joe Wilson who spent many years looking after it in his spare time. The pond is now looked after by the Durham Wildlife Trust whose members are in regular attendance. The Trust has its headquarters in a nearby building.

The Durham County Agricultural Society Show at Burnmoor has been a popular annual event for many years. This photograph was taken in 1982.

Viscount Lambton presenting a trophy at the Durham County Show, *circa* 1956.

There are many excellent public bridleways and
footpaths in the area. Here cyclists are on the stretch
of the Weardale Way running from Wapping Bridge
at Burnmoor to New Lambton.

The People's History

To find out more about this unique series of local history books – and to
receive a catalogue of the latest titles – send a large stamped addressed
envelope to:

**The People's History Ltd
Suite 1
Byron House
Seaham Grange Business Park
Seaham
County Durham
SR7 0PY**